P9-CLV-699

BIG BRANDS

SAMSUNG

THE BUSINESS BEHIND THE TECHNOLOGY

CATH SENKER

Lerner Publications • Minneapolis

contents

a global brand: Samsung today

Have you looked in an electronics store recently? If you glanced at the latest smartphones, you probably spotted a few Samsungs.

T he brand is well known for its classy cell phones—in 2013 one-third of the smartphones bought worldwide were Samsungs! Samsung has introduced us to futuristic devices such as the ultra-high-definition TV with its curved screen and the Gear S smartwatch, a slim, wearable smartphone with a keyboard, navigation system, music player, and personal fitness monitor. Samsung leads the world in the development of graphene, the super-thin touchscreen material of the future.

In 2014 Samsung was the world's largest electronics and information technology (IT) company for the fourth year in a row. Along with smartphones, it makes all kinds of electronics and electrical components, including TVs and memory chips. Based in South Korea, the company is also involved in skyscraper and factory construction, fashion, medicine, finance, and the petrochemical and hotel industries. In 2013 its revenue reached about $216 billion—more than rival tech companies HP, Siemens, and Apple.

The Samsung Galaxy S, one of the company's high-end smartphones

Samsung Sales and Earnings

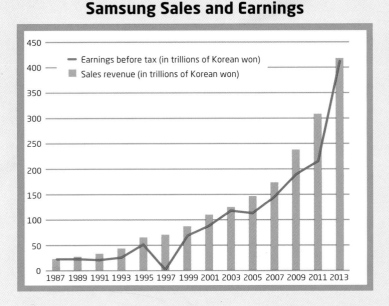

- Earnings before tax (in trillions of Korean won)
- Sales revenue (in trillions of Korean won)

(Chart x-axis: 1987, 1989, 1991, 1993, 1995, 1997, 1999, 2001, 2003, 2005, 2007, 2009, 2011, 2013; y-axis: 0 to 450)

In 2013 Samsung was ranked eighth in Interbrand's list of the world's most valuable brands. Samsung's excellent product designs are key to its success—it won nine design awards in 2013. The brand is also known for new innovations—it has clocked some world firsts, including the first full line of digital TVs. Because the brand is so powerful, Samsung is able to charge top prices. It sells its TVs, cell phones, and memory chips at higher prices than most of its competitors.

This book looks at how Samsung developed from a South Korean manufacturer of sugar, wool, and chemicals to become one of the top global electronics companies. What allowed it to become the market leader in producing memory chips? How did it overtake its rival Sony and manage to create smartphones to rival Apple's best-selling iPhones? What enables it to stay ahead of its competitors, and how likely is it to remain at the top of the fiercely competitive electronics market?

Business Matters
Brand value

Indications of brand value include how well brand-name products sell and the role of the brand in people's decision to buy them.

10:14
Tue, Feb 25

The Samsung Gear S smartwatch lets you use your phone hands-free.

A worker at the Samsung Electronics factory in the 1980s

Samsung starts out

In the early years, Samsung sold groceries.

Samsung was founded as a food export company by ambitious Korean businessman Byung-Chull Lee in 1938. In the mid-1950s after the Korean War (1950–1953) left Korea divided into North and South, Samsung became a major corporation. It manufactured sugar, flour, woolen fabric, and chemical fibers and sold financial services. In 1961 a military (army-run) government took power in South Korea. It supported Samsung's growth because it was good for building up the poor economy. Byung-Chull Lee became the richest man in South Korea.

Byung-Chull Lee
founder of Samsung

Byung-Chull Lee founded Samsung on the Japanese model. As chief executive officer (CEO), he was the "father" of the company, the employees were his "family," and there was harmony between them. Workers had a job for life, and the longer they worked for the company, the higher their salary was. This management model was later adapted to better suit the changing business environment.

Business Matters
Chaebols

Like other large South Korean companies, Samsung is a chaebol, or a company that is jointly owned by the founding family, private investors, and the various companies in the group.

In 1969 Byung-Chull Lee moved into the expanding electronics industry, founding Samsung Electronics and Sanyo-Samsung Electronics as part of the Samsung Group. Much of the technology, including the components, came from Japan, but from 1973 to 1974, oil prices quadrupled, damaging economies worldwide. Japan cut back much of its investment in Korea.

Byung-Chull Lee decided Samsung would manufacture its own components and took over Korea Semiconductor, which produced silicon chips. (There are two kinds of chips: the microprocessor, which has the instructions for computer programs, and the memory chip, which holds programs and information.) Samsung made great strides in the industry and in 1983 developed a high-speed memory chip. By then it had become South Korea's top company.

> **Samsung's research lab . . . reminded me of a dilapidated [run-down] high-school science classroom. But the work going on there intrigued me. They'd gather color televisions from every major company in the world . . . and were using them to design a model of their own.**
>
> **Ira Magaziner, a US business consultant who visited Samsung Electronics in 1977**

the global arena

In 1987 the military government in South Korea finally came to an end. Under the new government, people became wealthier and were eager to buy Samsung TVs, video recorders, and washing machines. Samsung also developed chemical, genetic engineering, and aircraft industries.

Kun-Hee Lee, who took over as Samsung's chairman in 1987, was not content with owning South Korea's biggest company—he wanted Samsung to be a global leader. To achieve his goal, he attempted to change the management style, encouraging young staff to join and to develop their own ideas. But senior managers who had worked at Samsung for many years didn't like this change. They wanted the juniors to obey instructions and were obsessed with increasing sales rather than developing new products.

Kun-Hee Lee decided on a fresh approach. Samsung would focus on its semiconductor industry, which required huge investment in equipment, technology, and expert staff. It presented an ideal opportunity to shift the way the business operated. In 1992 Samsung Electronics achieved its first important success, becoming the world's leading company in semiconductors. It developed the world's first 64MB DRAM, the most common form of random access memory (RAM) for computers.

Chairman Kun-Hee Lee focused on company strategy and left day-to-day decisions to his managers.

Samsung Aerospace was involved in the development of Lockheed Martin's F-16 fighter aircraft from 1997 to 2004.

Yet the Samsung Group's home appliances weren't doing as well. They achieved high sales in South Korea but were not in the first rank globally. In 1993 Kun-Hee watched a program on Samsung's in-house TV network and was appalled to see workers sawing washing machine lids by hand to make them fit properly. The products simply weren't good enough.

Building the Brand
PR stunts

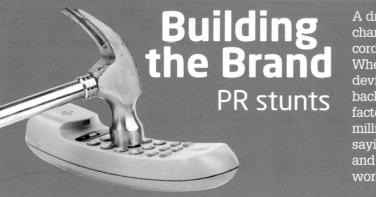

A dramatic PR stunt can draw attention to a business and change its image. In 1995 Samsung gave two thousand cordless phones to its employees as a New Year's gift. When many complained about the poor quality of the devices, Kun-Hee was furious. He asked them to bring back the phones. Then he had workers at the Samsung factory in Gumi bring their entire inventory—nearly $50 million worth of equipment—outside. Wearing headbands saying "Ensure quality," they smashed the faulty goods and set them on fire. This was Kun-Hee's message to the world that Samsung was determined to do better.

Jong-Yong Yun

Samsung Electronics chief executive officer (CEO), 1996–2008

Jong-Yong Yun steered Samsung through its most difficult decade. In 1998 he cut the company's debt by $13 billion in one year by selling off failing businesses, made operations more efficient, and cut costs. Jong-Yong Yun pushed for Samsung to embrace digital technology and produce high-quality consumer electronics, such as cell phones. He encouraged improved communications among the workforce by giving all staff portable computers and cell phones.

a new management style

In 1993 Kun-Hee Lee revealed his new management initiative to make Samsung a dominant global company. He switched the company's focus from the quantity to the quality of the goods produced.

A worker carries a placard bearing the face of Kun-Hee Lee at a protest about job losses at Samsung in 1998

Kun-Hee Lee introduced elements of the US business model. Staff now earned a salary based on their performance rather than how long they had worked for Samsung. Instead of vertical communication alone, from managers down to juniors, he encouraged horizontal communications among skilled workers at the same level. Everyone had to believe "change begins with me." Kun-Hee Lee also fostered a sense of crisis to keep everyone on their toes, foretelling that "all of Samsung's number-one products will disappear in 5 or 10 years." He pushed the company to adapt to change.

In 1997 an economic crisis hit East Asia. Samsung sold off unprofitable businesses and cut the workforce, which was considered a very "un-Korean" thing to do. Yet to push the business forward, it offered generous salaries to talented new staff, often from abroad.

A worker at Samsung's factory in Cikarang, Indonesia, in 2006

Samsung made huge investments in the research and development (R&D) of new products, picking areas that it hoped would be popular—cell phones, flat-panel computer monitors, and memory chips. The company had been behind in producing analog devices, but then it began focusing on new digital technologies. Entering the digital technology market early enabled the company to get ahead of its competitors. Overall, the strategy was successful, and Samsung became stronger than ever.

Business Matters
Research and development (R&D)

Companies carry out R&D to find new products and processes or to improve existing ones.

> " My coworkers spend a lot of time discussing each other's ideas to help each other develop them further. "
>
> Wesley Park, Samsung manager, 2005

Stages of Samsung's Growth

	Samsung's growth stages	Major events at Samsung
1938–mid-1950s	Foundation and establishment of Samsung's management system	Entry into manufacturing (1953-1954)
Mid-1950s–late 1960s	Growth into a large company	Diversification (electronics, heavy industry, and chemicals)
Late 1960s–late 1980s	Emerges as South Korea's leading company	Start of the semiconductor business
Late 1980s–present	Emerges as a world-class company	New management initiative (1993), restructuring (late 1990s), and has global number one products (in electronics, shipbuilding, heavy industry, and chemicals)

Building the Brand
Investing in manufacturing

Electronics companies succeeded in creating a market for their products. But there were many competing companies. How did Samsung stay ahead of the game? It developed the lead in a specialist area: memory chips. Samsung's huge investment in manufacturing facilities for memory chips allowed it to pull ahead of its rivals. Whatever new products were developed, they would require chips, and Samsung was the world leader, able to produce them in massive quantities.

In 1999 workers in a factory near Seoul make Samsung's latest product, the notebook computer.

Video cassette recorders (VCRs) in assembly at Samsung Electronics in 1990. VCRs allowed people to record TV programs, an innovation introduced widely in the 1980s.

creating a market for electronics

A big challenge for companies producing goods using new technologies is creating a market for them. In the late twentieth century, how did Samsung and other electronics companies persuade people to buy products they had never needed before?

Timing was key. Samsung Electronics was set up at the perfect moment. The supply of electricity was growing in South Korea in 1969. Koreans saw that people in the West had TVs, fridges, and fans, and they wanted them too. Samsung successfully took advantage of the availability of electricity to provide products that used it.

Likewise, Samsung's move into producing the semiconductors used in microprocessors was well timed. The development of microprocessors enabled computers to be made much smaller, in larger quantities, and far more cheaply than before. In the 1980s, these personal computers (PCs) were marketed to businesses. Companies such as Microsoft created software applications for businesses, including word processing programs and spreadsheets for accounting. Bill Gates, the cofounder of Microsoft, talked of a future where there would be "a computer on every desk." This prediction came true, and soon computers were an essential business tool.

From the mid-1990s, the Internet took off in wealthy countries, and people wanted to have PCs for entertainment as well as work. The price of computers fell further, and electronics companies pushed for everyone to have a computer at home. At this time, Samsung was a main supplier of computer components.

Business Matters
Advertising

When companies develop new technologies, they invest heavily in advertising to sell them. Computer companies were extraordinarily successful. The number of computers sold rose from 50,000 in 1975 to 134.7 million in 2000.

Computers have transformed publishing. Here, old books are scanned so that people can read them on a website.

building the Samsung brand

A visitor examines Samsung's brand-new flat-screen monitor at a trade show in the United States in 1996.

Kun-Hee Lee was determined to push the Samsung brand to the top. In the 1990s, he planned a global marketing campaign to make Samsung a household name in the West.

Samsung switched from making functional basics to focusing on high-value goods—items that consumers wanted on an emotional level. From 1995 it created desirable cell phones and flat-panel liquid crystal display (LCD) screens, which were lighter and more energy efficient than the older screens. This was Samsung's new premium-brand strategy. Would it work?

Samsung's head of marketing, Eric Kim, ran a test campaign in the United States in 2001, followed by a huge global marketing campaign. The company broke links with discount stores such as Walmart and made new alliances with higher-end independent stores, such as Best Buy and Sears. Customers started linking Samsung with quality goods. The company also tapped into the appeal of convergence products—devices with many electronic functions, such as color LCD phones and wireless handheld PCs. These moves succeeded in changing Samsung's image from an unfashionable South Korean brand to a popular company producing must-have items to rival Apple's sleek computers and iPods.

Building the Brand
Price skimming

In 2001 Samsung decided to try using a policy of price skimming—setting a relatively high price to boost profits. Well-known businesses frequently do this when they launch a new, premium-quality product. If consumers want the latest model, they'll be prepared to pay the price.

Samsung's stand at a trade fair in Las Vegas promotes the world's first curved Ultra-High-Definition TVs.

> "It was a change in 1996 by our chairman, who wanted to build a brand, not just a product. . . . We looked to the future to build the Samsung brand as iconic—one that everybody would want to have."
>
> Gregory Lee, global chief of marketing, 2005

Business Matters
Economy pricing

If you sell a product at a low price, more people may be eager to buy it. However, they may also think it's a poor-quality item. Also, you will make less profit per product sold and have less money to invest in the company.

Samsung

Samsung opted to raise its brand image by going head-to-head with its major competitor, Sony. In 2000 Japanese company Sony was Samsung's biggest rival in DRAMs, electronic appliances, and cell phones. Founded around the same time as Samsung, Sony was near the top of the electronics league—only Matsushita and Philips had higher sales. In 2000 Sony's sales were $70 billion—more than double Samsung's $28 billion. But Sony's growth had slowed to 5 percent per year while Samsung was expanding at a superfast 25 percent.

In 2001 Eric Kim announced that Samsung intended to overtake Sony within five years, and his goal hit the headlines around the world. The battle was

Eric Kim achieved his aim for Samsung to beat Sony within five years. He then resigned to take up a less stressful job.

SONY

Business Matters
The benefits of growth

Growth has two main advantages. A large company can buy materials in bulk for a low price. It can also spread costs such as marketing over the whole business—these are called economies of scale.

Sony

on! Hard work is very ingrained in South Korean culture, and the contest with Sony inspired workers at Samsung's main Suwon campus to work harder than ever. As well as phones, Samsung created portable DVD players and high-definition-ready LCD TVs—items that consumers bought because they were appealing rather than essential. Samsung's products flew out of stores. Market experts commented that by 2003, "young consumers were ogling Samsung cell phones and flat-panel TVs the way their parents once lusted after Sony products." Two years later, in 2005, Samsung had a higher brand value than Sony.

However, in 2007, business growth worldwide slowed. Samsung's fantastic growth rate faltered and profits fell. The company faced a new crisis.

Eric Kim
head of global marketing, 1999–2004

Korean American Eric Kim pushed for Samsung to sell products at higher prices. The contest with Sony was also his brainchild. In 2001 Kim came up with the DigitAll campaign. At that time, people in most countries believed that digital technology was just for wealthy users. Kim stressed that Samsung's digital technology could meet everyone's needs—both business and personal—and that investing in its products was worthwhile. This was already true in South Korea, where most people had advanced digital cell phones and Internet broadband access was the highest in the world. But it was a revolutionary idea in the United States.

17

overcoming recession and

Business Matters
Relocation

Wages are an enormous expense for every company. To cut costs, multinational companies frequently move their factories to countries where wages are lower—in Vietnam in 2007, workers earned around one-tenth of the pay of South Korean workers.

Everland, Korea's largest amusement park, is operated by Samsung.

scandal

s

amsung lost no time in adopting measures to survive the economic crisis. In 2007 Kun-Hee Lee announced restructuring (company reorganization) and cost-cutting plans. The company moved its main cell phone production facilities from South Korea to Vietnam, where labor costs were much lower.

Samsung was hit by another crisis in 2008—a political scandal. Kun-Hee Lee had begun to transfer his wealth to his son, Jae-Yong Lee, who was a major shareholder in Samsung Everland, South Korea's largest amusement park. In 2007 two directors of Everland were convicted for corrupt practices. They had sold Everland shares to Jae-Yong Lee at less than half the market value (which was illegal). The case damaged Samsung's good reputation, and Kun-Hee Lee was forced to resign. However, he became chairman again two years later.

Samsung overcame this scandal, and the company survived and thrived during the 2008 global economic crisis. Its market share of cell phones rose from 16 to 21 percent in one year, and it grabbed market shares from Nokia and Sony, keeping its high position despite the introduction of Apple's extremely popular iPhone in 2008. Samsung maintained its lead in producing components and was a brand that people wanted to own. It focused on its digital convergence strategy—integrating voice, text, and images on one device. For example, the 2012 Galaxy camera had a wireless connection so people could instantly upload their photos to share.

Building the Brand
Diversification—widening the product range

Big businesses prefer to spread their risks. Realizing that the electronics industry might not continue to be profitable, Kun-Hee Lee looked for new business opportunities in the 2010s. Samsung diversified into new industries, including biotechnology, pharmaceuticals, and medical equipment, and invested heavily in biosimilars, which are cheaper versions of brand-name biotechnology drugs. The company does nothing halfway—it aimed to become the principal pharmaceutical company in the world!

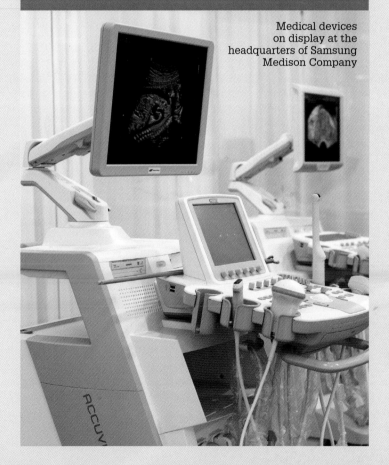

Medical devices on display at the headquarters of Samsung Medison Company

sponsorship

The Samsung Olympic Games sponsor truck accompanies the Olympic torch relay through British streets.

Top companies sponsor popular sports competitions to raise the profile of their business and encourage people to link their brand with these exciting events.

In 1998 Samsung became the official sponsor of communications equipment for the Olympic Games, providing wireless communications equipment. Using the Olympics global brand proved ideal for promoting the company worldwide. After the 2000 Olympic Games in Sydney, Australia, Samsung placed second in the world after Coca-Cola in brand awareness ranking.

In 2006 Samsung sponsored the Paralympics (Olympic Games for athletes with disabilities) to build its brand image. It also secured a deal to sponsor the shirts for English soccer team Chelsea from 2012 to 2015—every shirt worn by a team member or fan had the name *Samsung* emblazoned on the front.

Samsung uses ads based on Olympics themes in many markets around the world. For London 2012, soccer star David Beckham was the face of Samsung's Olympics advertising campaign, "Everyone's Olympic Games." The campaign spread the message that TV was no longer the main way to enjoy the Olympics. People could watch the games and share their favorite moments immediately on their new Samsung Galaxy phones, with special apps that allowed them to play 3-D and reality-based sports games with their friends.

Business Matters
Building brand affection

Companies look for ways to contribute to society to build affection for their brand. In 2014, Samsung funded the TV program *Launching People* in several countries. This recruited celebrities from the food, film, music, and photography worlds to mentor budding cooks, film directors, musicians, and photographers. The program featured Samsung tablets, phones, and cameras and aimed to show how Samsung technology could help talented people to achieve their dreams.

The launch of "Everyone's Olympic Games" in London, with David Beckham and equestrian Zara Phillips

> **Consumers are spending about eight minutes per visit on average on 'How Olympic Are You?'. This is double the time they spend on ordinary Samsung sites.**
>
> Ralph Santana, Samsung's chief marketing officer, noting the popularity of Samsung's Olympics-themed web pages in 2012

Business Matters

Planned obsolescence

Electronics companies tend to design products with a limited life so people often have to replace them. For example, software is constantly changing, so if you have an old computer, you can't install the latest software on it. The operating system may no longer be supported with security updates, so you are prone to computer viruses.

the consumer culture

Singer and Samsung ambassador, Lily Allen

Building the Brand
Targeting the youth market

In 2014 Samsung targeted the youth market for phones in the United Kingdom, using singer Lily Allen to market its new premium cell phone, the Galaxy Alpha. It aimed to show the smartphone being used by what it called "Alpha Britons," or high-profile British citizens who, according to Samsung, "embody the spirit of new modern Britain and its stylish youth culture." The marketing campaign was timed to compete with Apple's iPhone 6, which was released at the same time.

Do you really need a new phone each time an upgrade comes out? Cell phones have become a vital accessory, and electronics companies have persuaded many people that it's best to have the newest version with the latest features.

Businesses use social media to convince consumers to purchase new products. Samsung has had huge success on Facebook, promoting its major product launches to twenty-five million fans in Europe in 2013. Along with providing information about its devices, Samsung promotes two-way communication with fans, who can share their stories about Samsung purchases. This lets the company hear about any problems with its new releases and address them quickly.

The culture of constantly replacing our electronic gadgets has a cost to the environment, though—we create mountains of electronic waste, much of it containing toxic materials. Many materials can be reclaimed and recycled, but this takes money and resources. Samsung is trying to clean up its act. In 2012 it was seventh in the Greenpeace Guide to Greener Electronics. It is a leader in providing warranties and spare parts information to help extend product lifetimes. Yet few people use their gadgets for the full life span.

the **secrets** of **Samsung's success**

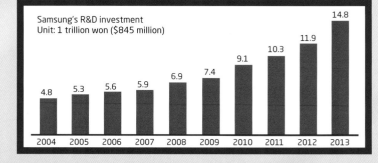

The Samsung booth at an electronics show in Las Vegas in 2014

Samsung's Research and Development Investments

Samsung's R&D investment
Unit: 1 trillion won ($845 million)

Year	Investment
2004	4.8
2005	5.3
2006	5.6
2007	5.9
2008	6.9
2009	7.4
2010	9.1
2011	10.3
2012	11.9
2013	14.8

Dong-Hoon Chang, executive vice president of Samsung Electronics, speaks at a digital technology meeting in 2013.

Business Matters
Co-opetition

Samsung has coined the term co-opetition—a mixture of competition and cooperation—to describe how it expects its employees to work. Businesses within the Samsung Group have to compete to outperform one another and compete with outside suppliers to deliver parts and materials. Yet each division has to create innovative products, so employees have to cooperate within their teams.

How does Samsung stay ahead of its competitors? In Korea, *ppali ppali* (quickly, quickly) is a common saying. Samsung has adopted the ppali ppali spirit, releasing products faster than its rivals. In the early 2000s, when camera phones were first being introduced, Japanese companies took an average of ten months to plan and release the phones, while Samsung completed the same process in half the time. The speed of production forms an essential part of the brand's message: if you want the latest innovation, buy Samsung.

The company is able to churn out new products speedily through "leapfrog" R&D. While it is designing a product, employees are already working on the next generation, the next-next generation, and even the one after that!

Production is fast because Samsung has its division headquarters (control center), major R&D, and manufacturing facilities in South Korean cities that are all within a radius of 18 miles (30 kilometers) of one another. The core parts of the Samsung Galaxy S5 phone are all made within the Samsung Group. Having all the sites close together allows for good communication between the different divisions and fast decision making. Experts from the R&D teams meet with the engineers from the manufacturing plant to discuss production issues, resolve any problems, and make changes right away.

In 2000 Samsung set out to lead the market in innovation—each company and division was expected to create a new product. To foster creativity, Samsung has Creative Labs (C-Labs) and a Creative Academy to encourage employees to come up with new ideas. On "C-Lab days," they demonstrate the results of their efforts. It was this drive for bright ideas that led to the development of LED TV and wireless broadband.

Samsung's future

Samsung phones on display in a shop in Thailand

Nothing is guaranteed in the fast-moving electronics business. Even market leaders can sink into crisis. The industry may change, leaving them behind while newcomers enter the market and forge ahead. In 2014 Samsung was faced with slowing demand and increased competition in the smartphone industry, and profits fell. The company needed to innovate constantly to survive. What could Samsung do to keep up its global position?

Samsung hasn't acquired as many other companies as its competitors. To adopt new technologies and products, it could invest more in other companies. A good way to foster innovation is to employ a wide range of employees with different skills. Experts have pointed out that the company increasingly hires more women, young, and international workers, but it could do more in this area and give them more responsibility.

More importantly, Samsung could work toward being a total solution provider, providing customers with integrated (well-linked) systems. Samsung has created excellent products, such as MPEG-4 (a way of making small files for sending video and images), digital TV, and IMT-2000 (mobile telecommunication standards for 3G mobile services), all of which were chosen for use worldwide. It also introduced Tizen, its own operating system, on smartphones in 2014.

Business Matters
Transnational companies (TNCs)

Samsung is a multinational company—it is based in its home country. Transnational companies have all their departments located in the places where suitable workers live or costs are low. This may not be the company's home country. Yet if Samsung became a TNC, it would lose the benefits of having its divisions close together.

However, it hasn't developed its own platform products—groups of software and products that have never been seen before. Apple did this by creating iTunes software and iPod music players. Yet Samsung is good at predicting trends and creating new products quickly. It developed the first graphene semiconductors and has a chance to lead the field with this breakthrough technology that could bring us a brand-new generation of must-have gadgets.

> By 2020, we seek to achieve annual sales of USD 400 billion while placing Samsung Electronics' overall brand value among the global top 5.
>
> **Samsung website**

market a new Samsung product

When you create a fantastic new product, you need to come up with a marketing strategy to sell it. Here's a sample marketing strategy for a possible device. Why not see if you can come up with your own idea for a Samsung product?

The Samsung Do-it-all

Building on the DigitAll idea, the Do-it-all combines all the functions of a smartphone, tablet, laptop, and camera on a superthin graphene computer that you can unroll to use wherever you are.

Stage 1: Work out your objectives
Step 1. Make sure they fit with your corporate strategy.
The Do-it-all fits perfectly with Samsung's strategy to be the first to bring out an innovative product.

Step 2. What do you hope to achieve?
Samsung's primary goal is to become the market leader. However, investing in this new technology may not bring in large profits immediately, so there are risks involved.

Stage 2: Product detail
Step 1. Product description and positioning
What is it?
The Do-it-all replaces the need for a separate computer, smartphone, and camera. Made from graphene, it can be rolled out to the size of a small laptop with a keyboard yet is as portable as a cell phone. A high-quality camera is included as standard.

An artist's impression of the structure of graphene

Who is it for?
People who buy high-end Samsung phones and fans with an interest in the latest technology.

How is it different from other products?
There is no computer or smartphone like it. If Samsung brings out the first model, it will have a huge competitive advantage.

What's the benefit?
Convenience and style: you have all your data, photos, and videos on one device.

What is the evidence to support your claims?
The Do-it-all will be thoroughly tested for durability to ensure it survives being dropped on the ground, rattling around in bags, and falling in water.

Step 2. What will it be used for?
It will have all the functions of laptops, smartphones, and digital cameras.

Step 3. How will it be different from other products?
No other product will offer so many functions in such a light format. It will be packaged in a unique case so that it can be carried in its rolled-up form.

Step 4. What is the pricing policy?
Samsung's aim will be to enhance the perception of the brand as a leader in innovation. In keeping with Samsung's general policy, prices will be high to reflect the quality of the product.

Step 5. What's the USP, or unique selling proposition (something that distinguishes this product from all others)?
It is the first product of its kind.

Stage 3: Understand the market
Step 1. Figure out which niche gives the best sales possibilities
At first, this premium-quality, high-priced product will be sold in the wealthiest markets with the most advanced technology, such as Japan, South Korea, the United States, Australia, and Europe.

Step 2. Create customer profiles
Market research will identify target customers by focusing on people who buy high-end phones and laptops, and electronics fans.

Step 3. How will you access customers?
Feature articles will be written for the technology and electronics press and all the social media used by target customers.

Stage 4: Check the competition
What competition is there likely to be?
Other prominent electronics companies such as Google and Apple are likely to produce mobile and wearable graphene devices.

Stage 5: Build your sales plan
Step 1. Key messages
Key messages for the target audience will play on the desirability of a graphene device on an emotional level—the opportunity to own a product at the forefront of technology—as well as the practicality and convenience of the Do-it-all.

Step 2. Promotion
The promotion strategy will include advertising in the press, on TV, at movie theaters, and on billboards. Samsung's public relations team will offer information about the Do-it-all. A Do-it-all website and a huge social media and mobile marketing campaign will be set up, and there will be promotions to engage customers, including competitions to win the new device.

Stage 6: Launch!
High-profile launch events involving celebrities will be held in all key target markets, timed for the pre-Christmas period to encourage the highest levels of sales.

glossary

analog
an electronic process used before digital processing

application
a program designed to do a particular job

biotechnology
the use of living cells and bacteria in industrial and scientific processes

chief executive officer (CEO)
the person at the top of a business

component
one of several parts of which something is made

corrupt
when someone uses their power to do dishonest or illegal things in return for money or to gain an advantage

digital
an electronic process using a system of receiving and sending information as a series of ones and zeros

division
a large and important unit or section of an organization

electronics
equipment that uses electronic technology, with many small parts, such as microprocessors and memory chips, which control and direct a small electric current

graphene
the strongest, lightest, and thinnest material known

initiative
a new plan for dealing with a problem or achieving a purpose

innovation
the introduction of new things, ideas, or ways of doing something

investment
putting money into a business in the hope of making more money

liquid crystal display (LCD)
A way of showing data in electronic equipment. An electric current is passed through a special liquid, and numbers and letters can be seen on a small screen.

manufacturing
the business or industry of producing goods in large quantities in factories

marketing
the activity of presenting, advertising, and selling a company's products in the best possible way

memory chip
a chip that holds data. RAM chips hold data temporarily while flash memory chips hold data permanently

mentor
to advise and train someone who has less experience

microprocessor
a small unit of a computer that has the instructions for computer programs

operating system
the "go between" that communicates between the software programs and the hardware (the parts of the computer) to make the computer work

premium
high quality

random access memory (RAM)
computer memory in which data can be changed or removed and can be looked at in any order

revenue
the money a company earns from the sale of goods and services

scandal
an event that people think is morally or legally wrong and causes public feelings of shock or anger

semiconductor
a device containing a solid substance that conducts electricity in particular conditions, used in electronics

shareholder
A company is divided into many equal units called shares. People can buy shares to own part of the company and receive a part of the profits—they are called shareholders.

software
the programs that run on a computer

sponsor
a company that helps to financially support a radio or television program or sporting event, usually in return for advertising

further information

Books

Sequeira, Michele. *Cell Phone Science: What Happens When You Call and Why*. Albuquerque: University of New Mexico Press, 2010.

Spilsbury, Louise, and Richard Spilsbury. *The Telephone*. Chicago: Heinemann, 2010.

Web

How Samsung Became the World's No. 1 Smartphone Maker
http://www.bloomberg.com/bw/articles/2013-03-28/how -samsung-became-the-worlds-no-dot-1-smartphone -maker

Samsung Website
http://www.samsung.com/us

13 Mind Blowing Facts about Samsung
http://www.businessinsider.com/mind-blowing-facts-about -samsung-2013-4

index

First American edition published in 2016 by Lerner Publishing Group, Inc.
First published in 2015 by Wayland

Lerner Publications Company
A division of Lerner Publishing Group, Inc.
241 First Avenue North
Minneapolis, MN 55401 USA

For reading levels and more information, look up this title at www.lernerbooks.com.

Main body text set in Glypha LT Std. Typeface provided by Adobe Systems.

Library of Congress Cataloging-in-Publication Data

Senker, Cath, author.
    Samsung : the business behind the technology / by Cath Senker.
        pages cm. — (Big brands)
    Includes bibliographical references and index.
    ISBN 978-1-5124-0591-0 (lb : alk. paper) — ISBN 978-1-5124-0595-8 (EB pdf)
    1. Samsong Chonja—Juvenile literature. 2. Electronic industries—Korea (South)—History—Juvenile literature. I. Title.
    HD9696.A3K77745 2016
    338.7'62138095195—dc23
2015033984

Manufactured in the United States of America
1 – VI – 12/31/15

Photo Acknowledgments
Cover: Nebojsa Markovic/Shutterstock.com (top), Caro/Photoshot (bottom); p1: JEON HEON-KYUN/epa/Corbis (top), Kobby Dagan/Shutterstock.com (bottom); p4: Zeynep Demir/Shutterstock.com; p5: Ivan Garcia/Shutterstock.com; p6: Patrick Robert/Sygma/CORBIS (top), Mohumed Maaidh/Wikicommons; p7: Janet Wishnetsky/CORBIS (right); p8: JUNG YEON-JE/AFP/Getty Images; p9: AirTeamImages (top), TakeStockPhotography/Shutterstock.com (bottom); p10: Sean Gallup/Getty Images (top), LEE JAE-WON/AFP/Getty Images (bottom); p11: Dimas Ardian/Getty Images, Stefan Chabluk (bottom); p12: Michel Setboun/Corbis (top), CHOO YOUN-KONG/AFP/Getty Images (bottom); p13: TopFoto/ImageWorks; p14: Gilles Mingasson/Hulton Archive/Getty Images; p15: Kobby Dagan/Shutterstock.com; p16: JUNG YEON-JE/AFP/Getty Images (top), REX/Sipa Press (bottom); p17: Kobby Dagan/Shutterstock.com; p18: Tanjala Gica/Shutterstock.com (top), JUNG YEON-JE/AFP/Getty Images (bottom); p19: SeongJoon Cho/Bloomberg via Getty Images; p20: Kumar Sriskandan/Alamy; p21: Fred Duval/FilmMagic; p22: Helga Esteb/Shutterstock.com; p23 REX/Image Broker; p24: JEON HEON-KYUN/epa/Corbis (top), Kobby Dagan/Shutterstock.com (bottom); p26: Tooykrub/Shutterstock.com, p27: www.exynox.net; p28: LAGUNA DESIGN/Science Photo Library/Corbis.